Christopher M James

Chosen ground

POEMS

MOSAÏQUEPRESS

Praise for **Chosen ground**

Christopher M James turns over memories as though meditating on an object in the hand, viewing from every perspective and sharing his observations leaving room for reflection. His vivid poems in Chosen Ground *shift between the personal and the universal using memorable imagery, cultural references, carefully layered metaphor, and alluring narrative. James takes us beyond ourselves geographically but also deep into bodily experience so that we both pan out and zoom in to what it is to be human. The snow scene of the cover reminds us how snow insulates, yet how it also makes sound, view, and the everyday, 'other' which is what James achieves in this moving collection.*

– MARIA ISAKOVA-BENNETT

Chosen ground is a generous selection from three unpublished pamphlets by James, and gives a strong sense of his range. As a poet, he mines his childhood to great effect in the first part where the visual exactness of his analogies is sometimes startlingly perfect. His explorations of otherness/other worlds extend to classical composers, to writers and other cultures, some of the best poems being about Thailand. His scope, as emotional as intellectual, is broad, satisfying, intriguing. Looking at paddy fields, 'their waters smudge/ a setting sun's inks. A hand/ has wiped leftover pigments/ on a cloth of sky.' Challenging, beautiful – this selection is excellent.

– BILL GREENWELL

In poems that span space and time, evoking many different places across the world and many different moments in life, from childhood to maturity, James employs striking metaphors that explore the complex weave of existence in poetry that is at once dynamic, vivid and contemplative. This is a collection to return to many times always finding fresh resonances in each line.

– COLIN PINK

In his quest for 'honesty's centimetre' James is always linguistically inquisitive. He uses pitch-perfect imagery that shifts perspective, creating resonances between things as if something unexpected has been clarified, giving these poems their wry insightfulness. Observant and concise, James scrutinises and explores our chosen ground, 'probing the riddle of what won't answer back.'

– REBECCA GETHIN

James writes: Your/ boyhood world globe was a skin/ encircling a lamp which you spun/ for all your tales to come/. These are the poems of that well-travelled life. There is something of the perpetual schoolboy in his indefatigable curiosity for the world. The poems are alive: skimmed stones whose small disturbances resonate long after they've passed. James brings a clear-eyed compassion and erudition to the many roads taken. He gifts us the certain knowledge that we will always have so much more to learn.

– MARTIN FIGURA

First published in 2025

MOSAÏQUE PRESS
Registered office:
Bank Gallery, High Street
Kenilworth, Warwickshire
CV8 1LY

Copyright © Christopher M James 2025

The right of the copyright holders to be identified as the authors of this work has been asserted in accordance with Section 77 of the Copyright, Designs and Patents Act 1998.

Cover illustration: Copyright © Arthouse Studio/Pexels 2025

ISBN 978-1-906852-72-6

Life...
he means to write one story
and writes another...

— JM Barrie

Contents

10 Acknowledgements

from **Coming in to land**

12 Old shots
14 Hooked
15 Duplicate
16 Fear of spiders
18 Reception
19 What I found
20 Sorcery
21 Aberfan
22 Round
24 Stories
25 Perfect pitch
26 Her first letter
27 The discipline
28 Alas, poor Yorick!
29 When Modest Mussorgsky looks like a drunk
30 Now thank we all our God
31 Ladder
32 My favourite part
33 The slight
34 Shut out
35 Just
36 Those telling gestures
38 Cranford Park

Epilogue:

43 Villain knell
44 Carrying you
46 Shapes

from **Oncoming faces**

51 Traces
52 Sea-horses
53 Night vision
54 We're all in someone else's story
55 Where does it come from?
56 Permeable
57 Maid in Thailand
58 Intravenous
60 Chiang Mai fire
61 Strays, Hua Hin
62 Village
63 Lazy fish
64 Point taken
66 Dermochelys coriacea
67 Yi Peng
68 Looking through construction site hoardings
69 Supply side
70 Polishing stone

from **Vanishing points**

- 75 Vanishing points
- 76 Leo drawing a moon
- 77 The very young
- 78 Stockholm Syndrome
- 80 Minka
- 81 Siren
- 82 Elementary particles
  1 Ravel at Montfort l'Amaury
  2 Reading Proust
  3 Shostakovich's fifteenth
  4 Spare a thought for Kafka
- 87 The Bipolar Coleridge
- 88 Marshes
- 90 Puffin, Húsavík
- 92 Thorsteinsskàli, Iceland
- 94 Back in my village
- 96 On things that fly
- 97 Sonnet
- 98 Ma 間

100 Mind the gap
101 All clear
102 Brain surgery on prime time
104 Shorthand Hotel
105 The jar
106 Simone Veil lays a foundation stone for a hospital, 1976
107 Golem
108 Trojan horses
109 True north
110 Cardea
111 The government of mud
112 Breakfast protocol
113 The pathetic fallacy
114 Crossed paths
115 Pantheon
116 Would you recall?
117 Confirm humanity
118 Coda

119 About the author

Acknowledgements

Many of these poems have appeared in the following poetry magazines/journals or online sites: *Acumen, Aesthetica, Amethyst Review, As above So below, Cerasus, Dream Catcher, French Literary Review, Ink, Sweat & Tears, London Grip, London Magazine, Magma, Orbis, Poetry Salzburg, Poetry Society.*

Other poems have been selected (some as prize winners) in the following competitions/literary awards and included in the published anthologies: AUB, Bailieborough, Bedford, Bridport, Canterbury Poet of the Year, Dempsey & Windle, Earlyworks, Fingal, Gloucester, Gregory O'Donoghue, Hastings Litfest, Indigo Dreams, Live Canon, NAWG, The Page is Printed, PENfro, Plough, Poets and Players, Poets meet politics, Red Shed, SiarScéal, South Downs/Binsted, Stroud, Troubadour, Verve, Welsh International, Wildfire Words, Wirral, WoLF, Yaffle, Yeovil. Other publishers – Cinnamon, Paper Swans, Ignition and Hedgehog – have also been helpful.

I would especially like to thank members of the French Online Stanza Group, and the Barnes and Chiswick Stanza for their judicious commentaries on a number of these poems, as well as Bill Greenwell for his enlightening poetry clinics.

The poems in *Chosen ground* have been selected from three unpublished pamphlets – *Coming in to land, Oncoming faces,* and *Vanishing points.*

CHRISTOPHER M JAMES,
Tamniès, July 2025

from **Coming in to land**

Old shots

The stained, crooked shoe box
ditches a pinch of snuff. Inside,
shades of light hazel, beeswax, born
as spurious black and white.

Some are stuck together
as families were entreated to do,
most curled with years, like
the bleached handwriting behind.

> One man is glaring,
> his wiry hair off to the side
> like a strong-blown flame
> of a hand-held torch;
>
> two sisters pose hands on hips
> in flapper dresses and plastered hair,
> bordering on drag
> from *Some Like It Hot*.
>
> Bathing trunks high-tide over bellies,
> ice-cream levered into whorls...
> Faraway, a sea's lost edge,
> rusted out by a paper clip mark.

Here's a studio print with serrated edges,
a fancy script at the bottom,
a paradise island backdrop,
serious money, serious pout.

A father unusually pushing a pram
with his tilted hat, his brooding Cagney spruce
not seeing a rickety fence behind,
giving the game away.

    Instinctively, this is where they stopped:
    a vegetable patch, brown tenement brick,
    grass in a park, a sand pit, an infant,
    a bucket, before bucket lists.

Shots to flag down unspoken thoughts
about what might well go missing:
a picture for this man in uniform
before he went to war,

    or this woman,
    confiscated by motherhood,
    who looks pretty,
    in the right play of light.

Hooked

I first learn about Relativity
when I flunk arithmetic
or am not picked for the team.

But if they do call my name,
it rings out, as if I'm coming in
to land from orbit. Then,

once a year, the green hills and fields
around our holiday let near Woolacombe
expand Space, lengthen Time.

At daybreak, Jimmy Tremayne
takes me to the deep ocean shore
with his lugworms and vernacular,

shows me how to cast out
as I would later for some memories.
When the wind wrestles his hair

into a hint of Einstein's, my rod
starts to bend miraculously, like Light
towards a whopping new planet.

Duplicate

First, wait until next morning
then after breakfast,
then everyone his turn. Don't tear

the paper, undo it carefully
as it has been mindfully wrapped.
Peel off the Sellotape, fold

the paper, there will be rainy days.
Show interest, give thanks twofold:
the gift, the thought behind,

pairing up
this prolonging of the pleasure,
this obstacle course to pleasure.

Fear of spiders

outstays drumming ghost trains,
cutthroats under beds,
those old creaking stairs.

A coquetry of instinct
to dread impossible enemies
more than likely prey ever could.

The anchorite in them
locks into air or corner stash,
a calling without ministry,

spins according to rite:
root attachments in limbo, diagonals
taut with grip, air's cliff-edge,

then inner crochets
orbiting a tiny drain of heart.
A syntax of prayer

blazing in the beauty of dew.
For what?
An off-chance the wind

would carry a whisper
to a dangling nerve,
and discard it, a hair's breadth

from pity but not pity.
Not the pity of the dark recesses
or webs in ourselves. At

each shudder, its whole body turns –
a positioning tank
for the pre-emptying.

It scurries over the rigging,
wraps a thrashing mass
into a packed mummy,

will later trigger
its one prime synapse,
retreating to the centre.

Reception

The two slender metal rods
pointed into space like on a Sputnik...
We sat it on top of the telly,
deep as a cave, but it scribbled
rupestrian signs then crossed them out.
We turned it, raised it with agility,
its gangly implausible starting point
threading to a muddled end.
Every week, my father on his knees
before a scrambled Richard Dimbleby
I waited for the Crackerjack contestants
to drop their prizes and cabbages
to the blast of a strangled goose.

Might it conduct stray lightning?
My mother, vaguely upbeat
reckoning in staple British
about fanciful weather, winds.
In spite of our acrobatics,
the simple, bare technicity of it –
like the missed signals of plain,
hopeful parenthood – seemed
somehow beyond our reach
on obscure wavelengths. Once,
we three managed to position it:
unsure of how, we stood there
barely daring to move.

What I found

The log's embers rise and wink
at the Andromeda constellation,

the shimmer makes a circle of our faces,
nerve-ends of the cosmos...

We touch a pierced secret,
our arms clamped around knees

in extinct dark. Our words
lean forward into stage asides.

One laughs, throws his head back
as if falling through a nebula.

Starry drift net, eaten with holes,
catches us all.

Sorcery

A charm from the book of spells. Since
those dummy runs and space creation,

the zone marking and possession play,
the closing down, pressing high, we forgot:

there was once a magic sponge land
where mud clung so hard to studs,

blending the laces into the body of the boot,
shin pads like growths, and the ball itself

zonking out in puddles, then growing
so big and burdened we pulled

our heads away. And tactics without
followers, which only the ball had

in its kicked-forwardness. We trooped off
spent, muddier, pounds heavier,

waddling to showers like penguins
on a slippery floor, our pretend wings

flapped out as if rescued,
soaring, defining.

Aberfan

The hillside had continued to spill
onto the hand-digging first responders.

Cliff Michelmore, in stark black and white,
his words threading, stitching,

beside himself with grief.
My mother never cried so much.

She'd had the two of us, had learnt
how children bury their riddles, how love

unearths them. Upstairs, my uninhabited bed,
cold as empty storage, safe as houses.

I gazed at the wall shadows, gently
swaying, memory-less, alive,

hearing all the voices calling out again
across the levelled land. Then

the moonlight's beautiful hanging hand
and the stars which called me lodger.

Round

Those days before child abuse
        I was let out early

to deliver thousands and read none,
        though the swing of the gates

sighed daily for scant news
        of the living. Every spring,

the half-light of a crenellated skyline,
        fortresses hiding in suburbs,

their decoy names beside doors:
        Chez nous, Bon repos, Xanadu...

In winter, the streetlamp beams
        wrapped scarce early risers

into the mist, one curt existence
        after another. And I,

stealthy in each season, for the sake
        of the dogs, their folly

and their fear of ghosts. I learnt
        the numbers, followed them

like at Sunday school, fathoming
        how to come close, how

to disappear, burying silence in steps,
    internalising the world.

None of *them* ever changed,
    not for another gospel,

not even at tinselled Christmas.
    Unbroken linearity

called *round* when done.
    It felt round as I pedalled home

when streets rustled like branches.
    Sometimes, my chain skipped.

Stories

Now, saw the frame corners and no wastage.
Wood doesn't grow on trees you know!

You've got positive ions and negative ions.
Remember, you can't have any... old... ions.

The quips surfaced over years
like continental drift, threw up pinnacles

for each new class. They cracked us up,
we who were told to straighten our ties.

When the bell rang, we filled the corridor
to the tuck shop, or plotted in the bike shed,

wondering if we would ever make something
out of the stories of our lives.

Perfect pitch

It's for her hidden inner ear
that it's necessary, a

spirit level in a tilt
of flesh, not

a poise set in limbo,
fit for pining's lock, stock

and barrel. It must fly
like a swallow's annotation

of evening's score, to honesty's
centimetre. Rachmaninov

had it, they say, stitched into
the lining of exile, and Boulez,

shuffling all his serial notes
like a deck of cards,

the house open, the key mislaid.
It's there in her entrance hall

between umbrella stand and mirror
that right song for her

not an insistent fugue
nor a clinched Amen.

Her first letter

is scented, palpable, close up,
like a night nurse monitoring

the finer points of how well
I'm wired up, her breath tight

through a rustle of words,
unfolding sheets. Here now's

a summer thought in a golden field
an ear of wheat in a flush of lips,

and there's a coin thumbed into air
snatching at the sun with a glint,

and there too, what she's heard
from her careful parents:

one of their hare and tortoise fables
dissecting the right speed of things.

The discipline

The museum display case
presents the object: *A discipline...*
From *discere*, to learn, Mr Slade says.
Why did he bring us here
if not for our own learning?

Mr Slade eyes us meaningfully
and says the same root
gave us *discipulus*, the pupil,
which fed into *disciple* – he
who follows the learning.

All that, before English-ness took over,
Chaucer no less, and the word came to mean
realms of knowledge – science, geometry
sovereign territories, escorting
darkness to some border. Soon

it shifted to verb, a side-kick to the *doctrina*.
To discipline: how to enforce what was
to be learnt. No longer a virtue itself,
but a step only in acquiring it.
A tightened sense of grip.

For now, I look through the glass
at this *discipline*, a medieval whip
of leather, tightened hemp and metal,
stark instrument of flagellation
for straying, heretical thoughts.

It lies as Exhibit 42. I lean forward
into how we cross the centuries:
as vibrant subjects for every hope,
as forsaken objects for each
of our shortcomings.

Alas, poor Yorick!

When it comes,
avoid the front seats upstairs,
get off the bus before your stop,
go down at the last moment.
Coarsen your accent.
Cover your wristwatch, look tied up
or just go for boring or constipated.
Avoid stupid questions – *What for?*
If some enjoy skipping around
a dropped body, let them.
Talk rubbish to a friend,
pretend he *is* a friend
to show how *not* there you are.
Don't overdo the blasé bit.
NEVER STARE! Above all,
avoid drawing attention to yourself.
If stuck at the bus stop
and they show up trawling
for eye contact, think
it's your future you're waiting for,
even if it's late
and half-full when it comes.
Know that one day you'll learn about
the genius of fear that defers war,
not the snap and knee-jerk of bullying.
You'll have another life
with second thoughts,
will learn metaphor and irony,
as when you imagine
two skinhead skulls, eyeball to
eyeball, for opposing bookends.

When Modest Mussorgsky looks like a drunk

with rosacea and pustules, fought-over hair and a wrestled life at 42,
in Repin's final portrait. When his very name means *restrained*.
When finding out is like trailing an endangered species, so
you stand thirty minutes on a cold, deserted platform,
and will come back in the dark with a ticket the size
of a bruise. When you've never heard trumpets.
When you're fifteen, unsettled, moonstruck, a
pinned-out exhibition yourself. When the
Great Gate of Kiev blows wide open
in a half-empty hall in Reading.

Now thank we all our God...

Early morning voices: a predictable
      quaver out, from the first attack,
lurching as trawlers do on the rollers.

That's boys for you, puberty breaking
      like waves in throats, though
the fine-voiced let that fact be known.

Twenty minutes to ride out each day
      for a supposed seamanship,
yet packed together like tinned fish

and incrementally shifting on feet from
      the loosening ballast of minds,
as if a whole boat was rolling. Who

would we call on to restore a song key,
      if ever the Sirens came?
Surely not the ones miming, cackling,

jolting as if already hitting rocks.
      Their eyes crossed the hall,
thoughts took an exit, but all those

on stage with a landlocked calling
      still searched for voices, as
an irked pianist banged ever harder.

Ladder

"And we want to go to heaven but we're always diggin' holes."
– CHRISTY MOORE

His headiness begins its swirl
from the tenth rung up
now the clogged gutter calls.

Light on gear but laden with
baggage: the school dropped out of,
the YOI, overstepped lines...

He'll look you straight into
your questioning eyes, admit
he got his calculations wrong,

then pace off up the street
wrestling with the maths these days
of two kids in a new equation,

following the black economy
to wherever ends may meet.
Up there possibly in the gutter,

his legs hitched like a frog's,
clinging to a chested intimacy
with wood. No Jacob,

with his rotting teeth and P45,
no dreamer, fearing more
the Buster-Keaton missing rung,

or below, another frame
from the past, a figure of authority –
a fat, whiskered cop perhaps

soles firmly rooted, elbows splayed
like a championship trophy,
prelude to a ludicrous, wacky chase.

My favourite part

Where do you come from? I'm from London. Which part?
All of me. – SPIKE MILLIGAN

... was when all of me, each time,
sank into a seat like a sultan
and bodies around rustled and closed
as darkness fell into our laps,

... was when Meryl Streep's arm bends back
after a throng of flamingos
to grip the vibrating edge
of a departed world,

or Chief Bromden
tossing a tub room control panel
through a staring window of opportunity
to the drum beat of his heart.

I was one of those new-born goslings –
project it across my blank brain
and never a probing *What next?* –
just following the run of

the motion picture,
its sinking in of lift-off. In
every cinema, my favourite part
was all of me plugged in,

charged, released,
keeping a frail peace
with my tank and windpipe body
which vanished,

until it came out sly
pretending not to be,
that sling of my restored arm
around her graceful frame.

The slight

You bite into a summer peach;
stars tingle in the palate's firmament.

You could be Abraham raising the knife
and not sinning, or a disheveled mongrel

trotting back, birds scattered into sky.
So many ways to immaculate sanctuary.

Not you now at home, living
forwards, understanding backwards,

growing like a tendril around words.
His blunt remark says

there's poetry to be flagged down,
as if you're stalled in a snowy forest

having left no clear note when setting out
of an intended route you still failed to follow,

unexpectedly caught off guard,
angry, uncaring, impregnable.

Shut out

A familiar click behind me
releasing a neat, trite silence.

My palms molest my back pockets
in two seconds flat. I'm swept along,

a stampede of conjectures,
as if I have a condition. Manic.

My forever rushing always leaves
half of me behind: a split personality

diagnosed here by a door. The door
has a mind of its own, a silent

voice and now over the phone
some god of a locksmith will quibble

about an urgent divine intervention.
By chance, an elderly neighbour

saves the day, poking acetate sheets
along the door's fine edge. At some point,

air takes its foot away. Panting, he gathers
his X-ray prints. So many of them.

I enter, wondering what else
I never knew about him.

Just

Just one night, before the coach to Istanbul,
in the flat of a friend of a guy. Brief decipher

pulling us to, sheets keeping us sealed in,
the young mother with a scar to show,

a birthmark in the hollow of her back
and breasts travelling light. Just a room

at a corridor's end in Goldhawk Road,
half-orange as the times and the bean bag.

In a corner a plush, yellowing polar bear,
slouched like a question mark between girlhood

and a destiny. Next day, just a coach window
to cushion the thoughts, and steps

to pile down with crocked legs at each
watering hole. Head-on lights near Graz

were our thrown-together eyes once more,
across a night. In a back pocket, a note

written neatly for a paper trail, proof
we had laid down, would not meet again,

a simple password of XXX's and hearts,
before a million codes waiting to be cracked.

Those telling gestures

her head cocked
breath frozen, fingers
target air, eyes spike
a phantom dartboard
for eye-liner

                      boy skimming stones
                      two three four five
                      boredom's recurring clones

he eyes the empty field outside,
a coupling of dogs, while
others revise beside him;   they try scrubbing it off
history teaches only   but graffiti
presences, absences   on the Circle line
orphanage of experience   just keeps coming
                                and going

    marooned beacon of a pub
    turfing out unsaintly patrons   Gdansk, principles
    they howl the world-founding   carried on shoulders
    canon of their youth;   chanting
    may turn out to be   thrust V signs
    plainsong   hinges of all lives

        serrated gob, lantern
        at the end of a long black tunnel,
        evolution's singular gratification
        for the deep-sea fish:
        no half-way, no bullying

the ticking clock is a country   to another, illness came
the book, a traveller   as a stray God
tiredness works the destination   to a last lighthouse keeper
from her hand   a light from afar, shrunk to
                                     a lamp in hand

she takes earth
to drop on coffin   a commentator's
rout of captivity,   tiny hesitation
lets it fall   did he stammer as a child?
improbable ballast   Wolverhampton Wanderers one
closed fist remains   Wigan one
sole weapon
of the oppressed
                            the powerless coach:
                            for victory or protest
                            his arm slices the air each time
                            throwing nothing

          light breeze rolls
          to its own lack elsewhere
          a waiter strolls   on a high wire
          between debit and credit   swallows in throng
          an arm semaphores thirst   have found
          earth's collaborate   the vital interval
                                       to be
                                       to belong

                    on church steps,
                    wedding guests
                    go up, go down
                    shake hands
                    nod like Japanese,
                    knitting lives

Cranford Park

It's personal. Like sticklebacks. Squatting to tadpoles. Racing sticks in the river, running along the bank. Grasshoppers dying in jars. Never could save them. Even such tiny appetites. Personal, like Tony Hancock's grave in St Dunstan's. Found it like an abandoned mattress thrown off the M4. Buried with his mother, there's a story. Personal, like the distant exclamation mark bodies you used to see walking there. Who drown in anecdotes on the memory wall. But close doesn't count. Suburbs are like purgatory that you never leave. Some cherish the twilight, sit on walls, escape to allotments. You say to people *What do you mean?* They know but don't answer back. Say *It's my life* and walk away. They're counting maybe, counting days before they hatch. Close doesn't count. I went away to college, to Wittgenstein who said private language does not exist. Convinced half of Britain. But he still cut off like Hancock, towards the end. Ruminative walks on the blowy coast of West Ireland. A cabin in Norway. But those who clung on the swings remember their sprouting wings. The taste of tea at the refreshment hut, the heaped clouds calling the evening in. Dogs were walked on weekdays. But at the Saturday five-a-side games no-one was covered in dog shit. Try understanding that. And nobody used – dared use – the showers. Every hot summer, the river pools dried up. When it rained again, minnows reappeared. Always. Like looking at a visitation. And the planes coming in low to Heathrow like refugees. Close, faraway. Telling you, you don't know. Near the church, the long, overgrown lines of walls in a wood. Where the Grey Lady used to appear. Or highwaymen disappear. They can't escape now, it's boxed in by motorways, main roads. Even the river Crane can't empty the rubbish that's dumped there. People used to swim. Used to be a manor house too. Like finding Richard III under a car park. What would he say now if he could? Then one long day, Mrs Maitland's murder. Her name ringing like tinnitus. Dr Jones did it my mother said and don't go there. Why would he do that? Went on for months. Year of the Sputnik yet still unsolved today: no DNA then, no private language they said, but we leave our own stardust everywhere. Most people don't want anyone looking for it. Guy who did it took it to the grave. Won't be turning over. Where's the full mapping out then? The accountability? We're not in this together. It's personal. Inextricable. Nights, I sleep on a hook, thrashing left right. Thoughts go smuggling in the park. Burying their booty. Baring their scars. So, you come to steal it with *Communication*. A moving target for you. But close doesn't count. Ha! No-one will take that from me and now I find it's all over internet.

Epilogue

Villain knell

My father has died. And not yet, for good.
I'm doing his thinking in the parlour of glass.
On the wall a certificate framed in wood.

He's well prepared, creases fall like overboard
from the drained, sealed, extinct mask.
My father has died. And not yet, for good.

He'd be embarrassed to look like he should,
like that, and that people had come to ask.
On the wall a certificate framed in wood.

This land of lost voices is groggily skewed
to drown in decorum with a hidden hip flask.
My father has died. And not yet, for good.

Picture it as he or Bruegel the Elder would:
the rustic detail, earnest toil, the village cast.
On the wall a certificate framed in wood.

I'm thinking for him, what his humour withstood.
We are an Investors in People company. Some task...
My father has died. And not yet, for good.
On the wall a certificate framed in wood.

Carrying you

Cars champing to overtake –
our driver knows the crematorium's
just-in-time – we arrive with you
at the last moment,

then shiver coatless, crunch
on gravel. We adjust our ties
pinched into silence,
face the waiting like shields.

It's all so hesitant to a figure
walking a dog on the grass
who glances at his watch, having
a bit part in a slow world. Then

a cold handle, a wedged shoulder,
that moment of touching
we never did before.
A step could wreak havoc

or a stone under a tight shoe,
a faltering corner or worse, the
turned heads that could shake us all
down to the ground, though

you are smaller than me
and I am not alone. They turn,
awash with familiar features, not
a single one with his regular face,

eyes yanking at our mooring ropes.
And I am held as much as you are
by this thing
that is to be done right.

I have returned from long exile;
so do words finish their lives
as gestures. Soon, you beside us,
I shall ride the way back,

still shouldering the evidence
I grew up with: how
things bind when close at hand,
or else go amiss.

Shapes

They left the book open, that either
I pick up, or never can put down.
Shapes the flesh grasped first:

round for elbow room,
a scatter map of place,
ellipses of desire, rows

of houses for non-template kids,
their candid square looks,
a few twisting arms. Or

the straight tug of an old war –
the rushed eating, the counting,
throwing nothing away – and

jagged hopes pieced together
like sideboard jigsaws
for chilly nights. But they'd seen,

years before, as if it came
from the sky, a hologram's
three dimensions,

its preposterous, implausible
oneness, and
wrote it in the book.

There were sudden bridges
raised like eyes over
reading glasses. And once,

an embrace through an ajar door,
their limbs coiling out of code.
But instinctively for photos

they posed flatly, delayingly,
as if half the book
was never to be read aloud

to make a circle virtuous.
Another page, I hone in:
two separate tracks –

growing up, growing old –
near-parallel lines, each searching
the other's direction.

from **Oncoming faces**

*Poems written during
an extended stay in Thailand*

Traces

Isaan, the vast rice-growing plateau in north-east Thailand

Endless paddies
stencil the land, enmesh the living.
Their waters smudge

a setting sun's inks. A hand
has wiped leftover pigments
on a cloth of sky.

A motorcycle
scratches the land
for epidermic dust, guessing

a low track, up to
a corrugated iron scar
of an outbuilding. What

pinprick of space is yours here?
The same as an old lady's,
squatting at a roadside. Your

boyhood world globe was a skin
encircling a lamp, which you spun
for all your tales to come. Now

you recall the rare times when,
dauntless, half-aware,
you tattooed the ready earth.

Sea-horses

I know of their seabed small talk
    in the small hours, as in prayer,
doing devoutly unto themselves. But
    they lie in the Chinese market,

tiny swollen bellies of famine babies
    minus the imploring eyes.
Too thin, too dry, too slight
    for pain and its trappings.

They mate front on, you tell me,
    with long foreplay, snouts
nearing snog, a heart shape of water
    quivering in between.

It's courtly love too: chessboard knights
    on Posidonia bedding. A
gallant male makes his opening gambit,
    carries the embryos. Coughing,

he gives birth and squiggles contort
    in critical-mass hundreds
to get a sibling through. How
    did you know all that?

And what do I know of you?
    I watch you twirling your hair
a single lock between your fingers,
    wonder how to win such things.

Night vision

Dead of night, outlying hotel.
I wake, jot down ideas in the bathroom
thinking headlong into the silence.
A mirror catches my searching look.
Later, somnolent, I hear you there
rubbing your Buddhist medallion
with toothbrush and paste
to stop it tarnishing. I listen
to your faint, soft strokes
and across the small town
neglected on the great plain
an occasional motorcycle drills
tiny holes for small attachments.
Coming back,
you curl onto my shoulder
an echo of my hopes
checking in one more time, just
to be sure, baggage and all
and proof of identity, that
at whatever gate we turn up at,
we are off to somewhere far.

We're all in someone else's story

Chiang Mai

When we moved in, our German neighbour was already dying. He watched us arriving from a window. Got up from his bed once to visit. Told us we were paying too much rent. And his wife was some sort of saint. And we should be sure to lock the gates when out. Told us he was the surviving, secret grandson of Hitler, his grandfather the carpenter at the Berghof in Obersalzberg. I listened, pocketed his narrative like an expired membership card. At his cremation, his tattooed biker friend helped to bear the coffin. But the usual firecrackers seemed oddly inappropriate.

Months later, he came back to me. I lay down and dreamed an old tale. He was the captain of my ship, gazing at the pin-cushion stars. We were en route to a faraway island. All the inhabitants there had it: one single eye in the middle of their foreheads. My plan was simple. Go to the island. Capture a few one-eyed specimens. Bring them back, sell them to a zoo. Make a sure fortune… But they must have seen me coming. When I landed, a group of one-eyed men emerged from the long grasses, accosted me. Took me captive. Sold me to the zoo. The zoo on the island.

Where does it come from?

for Chitpon

... Perhaps
When as schoolchildren, they wronged words
Their rubbers tearing the page,
What a monk once alluded to,
What a parent never did.

You woke, feeling sick.

... Perhaps
A chilling night, a tired prawn, a dearth of sleep.
What was the cause?
Not clear.

He came with food, placed it beside you.
Made a vomit bucket, then watched.
Came back with pills. Again, with drinks,
An extra blanket. Again, to ask questions
When all you wanted to do was sleep.

I couldn't tell him that
With my tonic lapses and grunt words,
So, he poured his liquid meaning
Into my blanks, moulding me
Into fool's gold.

... Perhaps
The thread of compassion
Stitching diminutive pearls, sequins
Into any moment's passing....

We said goodbye the next day
You right as rain. He approached,
Immeasurably grateful to me,
Threw his arms around
My parked body.

Permeable

Crowds spill over
holding bowls fragranced
with flame of the wood, yellow
gardenia, cape jasmine
cleansing the gold-leaf statues
of Buddha for this New Year.

I pitch forward to the front
to come out in the wash, use
two lotus flower stems to fleck
the water drops awkwardly,
fastidiously, a pointillist painter
honing in, out, in,

amidst the spirited jostling.
But an earnest lady to my left
lightly dabs the stems like swabs,
as if for the burns patient
she might have been, the
sudden nurse she is becoming.

Maid in Thailand

She missed a Tuesday, when the molten sun
poured into the crooked mould of the streets.

Came later, wrestling with her scooter,
as if easing a stick from a spirited dog.

It was because of the devotions for his dead body,
monks, food and all, her husband well accompanied,

the good thoughts done – but his motorcycle
a write-off – and that's life, so to speak.

> Another day, an early morning road: the sun's
> low hunched shoulder is sparring with the fields
>
> where a droop-headed buffalo plods like trust.
> I narrowly miss the four-by-four careening off
>
> to the side into my lane – a fanciful coleopteron
> it seems, mirrors barely a concept even.
>
> Breathless, I pull over, as admiring as I am
> shaken, that suns burn into different days,

and they rarely look behind.
In cars. Or in life.

Intravenous

They brought you in to ask how
your body fits into the cosmos.

Silhouettes out front take last drags,
stub them out. Inside,

the corridors are like creeks;
you hear their landing craft nearing

bearing molecular nutrients
to lodge on the banks of your flesh.

Arm stretched out like a jetty,
you lie back: the ceiling is cream.

Capillaries take hold like mangroves.
The sixty per cent ocean of you

is dormant, deaf, and you recall
the communion wafers

of childhood melting on
your tongue, as you wondered

what your hoped-for God
might end up hearing.

Imagine though, meanders of time
in the oxbow tubes, and

how you love the hands of man
in their right take on nature.

They will steer you out
of the forest of your body

where you thought you didn't rule
or weren't answerable, but when

the nurse smiles, pulls away from
your pale skin, you're back outside

finding your fingerprints
in all the felled tree rings.

Chiang Mai fire

A mile away,
a farmer is staking out ground
as if planting flags.

Fades in, out, in,
an unopposed intention
in a smoky picture frame.

What's no longer forest
shifts to farmland, or is buildable.
The slope is reeking black,

trees are burning, our hopes too.
Floods will not come as we wish
or cleanse the stockpiled seas.

We know, balk, just drive
our usual credits into the ground,
jet lag our sense of time,

shadows of ourselves, yet
ourselves wholly.
Like that distant farmer:

the sound of hammering
then, misaligned,
the sight of numb violence.

Strays, Hua Hin

Well, so-called strays, you said.
    They criss-cross, regroup,
    trot suddenly lock-eyed
stirred by some juiced discharge,
    an advancing jaw with a fresh
    objection. I know them best
deflated on their sides
    one's drooping teats
    coating the tarmac,
too un-puppyish to truly like.
    When the sun takes a turn
    they rise slowly,
front legs first, learning to walk again.
    A known quantity
    in a limited liability world,
prompting only our soft options
    of jamming brakes, walking by,
    feigning indifference.
Monks alone
    trail a hand as they pass,
    for them to whiff
the promise of *consequences*
    as if intriguing a future return.
    But at night
they're on a home run
    along the unlit road to a restaurant.
    You often told me
spirits make up the whole picture, things
    go around. Here now,
    ocular glints beyond my beams
see me guessing them;
    I lean forward
    in our car's solipsism,
wary of harm I could do to them,
    or by ricochet you say,
    what might befall me.

Village

The sun's long, insistent soliloquy…
we wait for the applause of rain

on the roofs. Or a special event:
a villager returning from America,

whose cities are racked with purpose,
bearing gifts for case-sensitive relatives:

tablets, smartphones, touch screens.
But Calling out is their *Bluetooth*,

and they voice their *likes* by the way
they crowd around, look on. *Browsing?*

How often they walk past.
Their *downloads?* Where they come to sit,

while kids on red earth hog the ball,
kick up dust like tinder sparks

and a buffalo plods by on a track
like a pulse in a cochlea.

Follow the trail of shoes, for
the sleeping rough part of being alive.

How do they grow, live, marry,
tip over into certainty? But

I sense the unobtrusive stories
when the moon is dry rind –

high, gouged out, wasted –
and silent fields backdrop deft space,

where an unknown howling dog
yaps a boundary.

Lazy fish

Teenagers sink like weights into chairs,
drown in phones, only surface to groom
selfie postures they electronically share.
Their curt, sparse words are strewn

around the group as in-jokes, to ensure
they are close and safe from adult ways.
When one spots the lake's round contours
sucking the rippled surface, heads raise

in unison, take pellets by handfuls, hone in
to taunt the Koi to a frenzy. No hunting pike
those waiting carp, sounding depths of human
resolve and approachability, like for like.

point taken

Luang Phor Sod Dhammakayaram Temple, Ratchaburi

so
do i collapse in my finery
at the first notes of *Nessun Dorma*
           or stir a memory to sip courage
           from a pot of years
or have my crowd raise its arm
for justice in a street

he tells me
        pain is but a book to be read

the dagger in my back does not belong there
        it's a roaming radio wave
        adjust the dial
how do i know this?
each time it shifts slightly
unaware what it's looking for
a random frisking at some frontier
        and yes let it rummage
        i've packed my own bags
        am bringing nothing in
rather i'll do the asking
        what is the pain looking for
        what will it say when it's found
        nothing
each question has it chasing ghosts
my mind now
a moving target

pain is a thief, he says
as i sit awhile cross-legged before him

                and posture the law

straighten up
like the drained rice-planters crammed   in
                an open toyota pickup truck
watching the landscape behind
fall softly away

Dermochelys coriacea

They came in flip-flops
for the promised night,
aware she was not a Cetacean
beaching, buckled
under its own weight,
its echolocation hijacked.

In the dark, they see her
coming up on crutches
uneven Morse surges on
Mayday sand, the head only
outstretching the shell
or the memory of frigates.

They become looters
under a masked moon,
their phone beams
catching her red-flippered
in the raw act, leering
into the busted night

with a burst, panting lung.
Keyhole apertures probe
the hollow where dank,
dented ping-pong balls drop,
as if born of drifting plastic,
hoodwinking as jellyfish.

Her ligneous jaw
hinges like a clapboard
the neck only in a slow thrash.
She is an old child, her eyes
streaming on skin rind. There
goes the salt in the wound.

Yi Peng

Festival of lanterns

They've stopped all flights for the night.
It's as troubling as a skein of geese.

Through the syntax of streets, onto the bridge,
the sky's glut of punctuation smudges

in the river's scrawls. Crowds look up
as if for a coming of extra-terrestrials.

Yours may end up on the planet of a stranger's
garden or be dropped at a roadside:

that flattened stencil paper you hold
with wire rings and hardened wax engine,

made big and round for the launch.
You'll do it according to the mind's

simplest slide rule: make a wish, send it skyward.
Stand now your chosen ground, stretch

its accordion skin, light the wick, and the trick
is to hold it so low and firm by its thin edge

that the stored heat hoists it up like it means it,
releasing the past inside of you.

Silent couples drink in the beautiful pearled sky,
each tracking far away their own single lantern,

wavering or headstrong like offspring
until lost to others or out of sight.

Looking through construction site hoardings

Bangkok

There's a sand mafia controlling supply.
The hungrier they are, the more sky

devoured. Investors imagine fast lifts
straight up to glory. Yet the greedy

reincarnate as starving ghosts, they say here,
with large hands and with mouths so tiny

no food can pass. Forever wanting more,
they stomp and rage, come below dogs even

in the karma hierarchy of the next life.
And here's another stamped footprint,

trampling a city's finesse. Across
the half-completed condo entrance,

my eyes follow a trail of light paws,
set firm in hardened concrete.

Supply side

The girls have gone through
all the filters – don't ask which –

adorning themselves to be looted
by the marinating silhouettes.

Home is but a theory about place,
where a yearning memory sticks,

a family echoes. Here they know
they don't call the shots but try

just the same, waving over
the standing-looking ones,

the back-and-forth ones pretending,
who size up their precipice of doubts.

Are they hoping for a solitary polar star,
or simply an asterisked footnote to love?

Or are two separate lifelines
merely facing up the passing years –

men, ready geared for the long
opening hours of make-believe,

or ladies, open for chance ways out,
that night after dark night shuts?

Polishing stone

The wind's up,
the longboats dragged in,
children sit, legs dangling

watch the spray
lashing the furrowed beach.
Three days like this. I'd hoped

for a boat's staccato thuds
around the long promontory, pushing up
as if levering off a paint-tin lid,

not the default mountain path
our legs now stab
through stone, bush and cacti.

Below, the beach coconut trees ripple
like ribbons for rhythmical gymnasts
in some obscure contest. Higher up

winds start to lose their minds.
How far have we come? How far to go?
Counting. Unsure what it is we count.

Years of footwear have polished
the stone track as memories do
for unevenly dealt hands.

And each rare oncoming face
seems to loosen a fragment of humanity
from the cliff of its past,

as we straighten up,
trade affable words,
unfailingly breathless.

from **Vanishing points**

Vanishing points

All nature seems to be pointing
importantly to a supposed prop
      on a remote shelf. An artist
walks the promontories of his eye
into found perspective. Long ago,
the before-Giotto faces and bodies
were layered up emphatically flat
      in an urgent foreground,
exalting reality as heavenly,
the mind assigned so little space.

No lesser artists here: you, me
the carpenter loyal to the grain
      the plumber his gradients,
the train driver's one straight line, as
he calls to mind his schoolboy love
or stillborn child whose name haunts
like an abandoned station, from where
      they lead day after day, to how –
somehow – they all shall meet up,
bags in hand, at the buffer of infinity.

Leo drawing a moon

The crayon poised to drown
    in the sea of tranquillity
or dropped over an enchanted well.
    With the moon, he'll come

to see the soul of a forest
    the dream of a madman
the hollow of a pillow.
    He scratches at the sky,

seismographs an urge, fills in the moon
    piecemeal, as pockmarked
as the living. Parents behold
    his slow incarnation:

aren't they right to believe they
    are half-gods now, can pin up
his work on a conspicuous wall
    as if it is their very own?

Where it hangs like a clock, faintly
    ticking within the stick people,
the trapezoidal house, a blob
    of a tree, a loved dog.

The very young

are swarming purposefully
over the paths outside,
    pedalling hard into
    their own thoughts, squatting –
the introverts – to slugs.

We know them for knowing ourselves,
for the braille of their hugs,
    the vernacular of their tears,
    how their cravings alight
on the thinnest of nothings.

Each miracle from a long glint in eyes
one warm summer evening.
    The earth is at it, too:
    wings fluttering, geese
tripping over stampedes of baby fans.

Is it a boy or a girl? we asked,
leaning into the scan. We'd heard
    from nature: one extra degree alone
    would bring out the feminine
in a crocodile or a turtle.

Though later, when we send them to
the *Stool of Don't Want To!!!* they buck,
    sulk and bawl their punishment of us.
    We cannot stop them
coming and becoming,

pouring into our space
we'd set up to be safe, when
    we thought we'd spoken our mind
    with one voice
about things as they are.

Stockholm Syndrome

A study of news reports showed that there were 638 selfie deaths reported globally in the ten years from 2011 to 2021.

Late in the day at a Yosemite overlook,
    a couple went softly over the top,
were found double-jointed below, their
    clifftop camera staring into space.

A helicopter flew the wild terrain
    below Taft Point, scanning the trees
for a flash of her pink dyed hair which,
    falling, crossed a goshawk's eye.

They must have been like many,
    rehearsing life once more into purpose,
grateful witnesses ever since
    their early years in Kerala,

but distracted by living's whirr
    from what to hang on to, how
to look decently back at oneself
    and not be taken hostage by

apertures and selfie sticks. Here
    online is another and another:
one rashly twirling a pistol, one more
    leaning out much too far

from a hurtling train.
    None of those lost were
the crane scalers, statue climbers,
    the skyscraper spidermen,

daredevils on one leg high up
    on an ultimate beam, but
only folk with no catch to them,
    whose hearts used to go out

to gashed, panting turtles,
    dolphins ensnared in nets
or a panicked deer, cornered
    on a motorway.

Minka*

A bullet train scratches out the thin street cracks.
Momentary neons betray the calligraphy of lives
whose space is counted in tatami mats, whose
silence casts about for lineage. In the mountains,
time pretends to go both ways: the cryptomeria
and hinoki cypress planks stare over the shoulders
of the master craftsman. He cuts into his own body,
each time reassembled, drawing the wood planer
into his viscera, his saw teeth angled to purr
by a pulling motion alone, towards, never away.

* *traditional Japanese wooden houses*

Siren

Alarmed at missing a cue,
it clamours for space, through
the narrow cochlea of the street,

howling to cower cars,
white coats ready inside to ram chests,
encircle mouths, lean into

prostrate conch shell heads. At
the corner, it stops. There,
now maestro hands are called for

to conduct the rescue with swabs,
drips or tourniquets, after
the ablutions of tuning up, as if

to groom an answer out of silence
for an opening bar. *Can you
hear me, sir? Can you hear me?*

They crouch and shrink to
the damage done, unlike the part-bird
Sirens of old over rough seas,

singing the sweetest of songs,
to lure onto rocks, when even the wax
the sailors plugged in their ears

dissolved under a wick of skull.
Now the throat manages a low groan:
a timely corner rescue it seems

or is that just us – haphazard, silent
onlookers – wishing to be less mortal,
and beautifully whole again?

Elementary Particles

1 Ravel at Montfort l'Amaury
the genius of the outline... – PIERRE BOULEZ

His mother's key signature:
curled clef of body, stave of cord.
Add two sticking plaster sharps to the nose tube.
There. One D Major existence. Then a tiny
raised walnut fist... *Concerto for the left hand?*

The church bell jingles in the china cups,
the bird-track Asian prints stare back.
Search the miniatures say the porcelains.
Ask the porcelains reply the miniatures.
Who knows? shrug the glib automatons.

    Climbing down the cramped staircase
    your body curls to a question mark,
    on the edge of impeccable lost secrets:

him being part-Minor after *Couperin's Tomb* –
there's a war and a mother in there too –
or bewitched years later, his mind running
crescendo eighteen times for a Russian dancer.

Here now, the insomniac, folded
in a gold Louis chair at first birdsong
when Mme Révelot trays in the breakfast.

    Search among the bibelots,
    the chosen *chinoiseries* and placed figurines,
    the surgical personal grooming instruments
    their unfathomable precision.

Search the caged air. The spleen
you brush past in the narrow corridor,
shadows stretched like a cape in an alcove.
Search. Unravel Maurice.

He never married. No known affairs.
No straying. When he died,
Mme Révelot stayed on. Her gone,
Mme Céleste Albaret moved in –
Proust's housekeeper.

    The ladies twirled their feather dusters –
    solitary conductors, key signatures –
    in labour for years.

2 Reading Proust

On his planet
    you expect to see
his swaying cork-lined carriage
    docking from space
he steps out coughing
    a silk handkerchief to his mouth
waving you away with the other hand
    to some trifles of remoteness
that belong to you:
    your first *Doctor Who* psychedelics,
those spinning sound waves, stoned or sloshed
    Daleks thrusting their sink plungers
that eye on a stalk.
    Simply carrying in his bags
will take you to a constellation –
    the bow-tie Orion perhaps? –
through the lanes of Combray.
    He'll eat a cake like a cosmos.
When he stretches to tie shoe laces
    his grandmother dies instantly again
for the first time.
    Every texture a memorial.

Once in the drawing-room
    the taffeta coat falls
onto the fainting couch
    as if a horde of confessions
was jockeying for position
    before a spiralled notebook
to put his own stop to child's play.
    You think it's an end
it's barely the beginning: just one hour
    reclining in that gravitational field –
because he couldn't sleep that first night –
    one hundred
of our earthling years.

3 Shostakovich's fifteenth
"the hum and clatter of hospital machines" – TOM SERVICE

Violins arch skywards,
percussions rattle bones...

the loose change of his body –
in whose pocket? – is art unplugging

the halo from its own dear cause.
He's on a high wire, nervous

as always, his pole a quill
scratching the rarefied air,

quoting others in homage, with
no more scores to settle. Petrograd's

young man with Lenin's cap,
ever officially optimistic, a paragon

for the motherland, though it filled
with crow's feet, medals like dentures,

thick uniforms colluding in tribunes.
There's crowd here still, only

his simpleton has changed, and music's
the art of the drunk sobered up.

They named an asteroid after him
but how high would he go, and

who dare ask: what of God?
Listen – the halting breaths, spaces,

ledge by ledge, the question
there at the end.

4 Spare a thought for Kafka
And yet. No 'and yet'. – DIARIES, JUNE 12TH 1923, FINAL ENTRY

They say a full stop quits,
monosyllables go to ground,
quotation marks forgive.

There, a century's *angst*,
darting, buzzing around
the fly-paper of existence,
that he had the urgency to seize
and send to what looked like
a sail: the page.

He felt arthropod from the start,
waking from *uneasy dreams*.
Gregor!

Segmented body, jointed appendages
but no feet caught, ever:

a stern father, petrifying women,
Cratchit-like office work, phobias,
his "sin" of German-ness in Prague
and Jewishness in the Absolute,
existential dread,
there he goes flying again...

I'm surprised;
it's taken a hundred years
for some to be told
there's a Mr Kafka waiting outside
who's been waving a safe conduct pass
at a pen pusher, protesting that
from childhood on,
memory is a landslide.

Informed of his exoskeleton,
we decide finally to break in.
A century
of collective dark violence behind us,
do we proceed to question him.

The Bipolar Coleridge

That which suits a part infects the whole – ODE TO DEJECTION

The bird that carried him to his mother's crotch
abandoned him to gravity. But his lineage *was* part-bird,

slapping water with arm-wings each time she bathed him.
Growing, he was never sure why the earthly cockerel

ends up stranded on the church spire, buffeted by gusts, as
the soaring eagle is crushed by the Book down in the pulpit.

That first March day he found the speckled blue eggs
of the blackbird, pierced two holes to blow them dry

and wrapped them in cotton, he became seasonal too,
steered by brain crystals. A swallow announced his spring,

but starlings showed him the drain in the sky, how
to screech, chatter and trill, how to rattle your heart out.

Oh my! The louder he was, the more obvious he became.
He watched a winter robin hop on to a swing gate

of how luck turns. That was the moment he resolved
to spurn air, brave the earth, a worldly poet, and flow

like an enduring ocean current. But when he was all at sea
an albatross trailed him for vast days on end.

Marshes

Wind combs the cordgrass
parting the hair on a lost sea's scalp.
Drops of rain punctuate

the half-light with air quotes.
From this distance, we listen for
the cries of snipes feeling their way,

foraging mud's tunnels.
A peewit's call of distress
is emptied of all irony.

A sole heron dares a neck.
Far down the path
a birdwatcher sifts the evidence;

his hands rise, drop, rise
as if rubbing his eyes, unsure.
He leans forward, peering

through a keyhole into sky.
An artist, with a court
of canvasses and paints,

pares down the patterns of light,
probing the riddle
of what won't answer back.

Must he add the birds from memory?
Is he searching for
nature's vanishing point?

Our side, we think
we're close to a stash of plovers,
but their world too

is thin-skinned now:
we crouch, our over-whispering
still bulky as a bowling ball,

sends one wader alone,
snappish into air
and away.

Puffin, Húsavík

Like the coastal hamlet you're from
his ends light up first:
arctic clownery from nose

to oversized shoes, even
here in full daytime.
He's cocksure on a rock

for the joke is on you. You spent
a morning looking for those fish
dangling from his bolt-cutter beak.

You wonder how a bird
with a head stuck in a Tango can
and wings like toddlers' paddles

can out-perform your rocking boat
or the great sagas of your learning.
Back on shore

in the straightjacket cold
among the pockmarked rocks,
you observe

his filled-out cheeks,
his blepharoplastied eyes.
xmxmmxx xmxmxmxmx xmxmxmmx!

To seduce the capelin and herring
in the sea's low dive of a nightclub,
using water as a comb.

Don't go after him or his like
to grab the spoils; he winks back,
will be here when you're gone,

when the prankster
of a stowaway sun punchlines
who will be first, who'll be last.

Thorsteinsskàli, Iceland

*"Outlaws fled into the broad expanses of the harsh Icelandic interior...
The general populace came to fear the vast backlands as the haunt of
supernatural evil."* – LONELY PLANET

Blistered-lipped, they ate their horses,
angelica root, a crawling hyphen on stone.

Nights, the locked sky swung as gently
as pendants around their necks

when they rocked like autists on lava flows
and gripped their shorn translation of life.

Escaping their revenge killings... inland,
a prison already, why build more?

Smouldering came late to the sky's edge –
too winter long, too summer short, though

bright enough to pick lice from one's clothing –
and snow shrank to laid-out body bags.

How often they scanned the thin horizon,
veins drumming like full regiments,

their optic nerves twitching, jarring –
enough to go blind with the focusing.

Forefathers came, but what grew here
were men remembering being children

elsewhere. Family trees alone were planted,
the others cut. Then one plain day

the only way onwards was into myth,
following a cortege of shadows

across the vast, cold hinterland, shadows
of killed brothers, of starved kin,

their minds grinding resentments like bones
into the tiniest of fragments. Earth's

anger erupted when glaciers blackened,
the tightrope of hunger made them

narrower and blinder. On rare days, the
northern lights' soundless folds of silk

crushed them by beauty
as they fell to their knees.

Back in my village

they talk a lot in shops, fill in the gaps,
say what they know to catch

what they don't. The same way
they count coins when paying,

searching a name like five cents
deep in a pocket. The inside story?

The main street. Shopkeepers
call out to each other but whisper

about the back-room apothecaries
of margins. Cars are parked askew

like intended slips of the tongue,
and making light work of it, I've

blocked an exit, hazard lights on.
That's me in the local dialect.

In the baker's, the tight queue
is eyeing breads and pastries,

puckering lips for the wind instruments
they are. I look for my *viennoiseries*

for this morning ritual, to prove
there is causality. And since

I am shuffling on my feet,
barely inside, in the line's tail,

and joy is a scent in the air,
a promised land, a slippery eel,

the slide-door's tireless beam
picks me out, as

its finely-tuned mandible
opens, closes, opens.

On things that fly

The first thud:
a green woodpecker
inert on the tiles

a drip of blood at its beak
repellent to the touch.
Then a redstart, stunned

it seemed, laid out on the grass.
And my pointless waiting.
A year back, we left the city

and its illusions behind –
the strides of advancement,
a career on stilts –

for this house in a green valley
where time disentangles
like the long thread of road

to our door. I wonder
the song to sing. I wonder
the birds in me:

a high skein of geese
seen only yesterday, or
that woodpecker guessing

the beautiful blue pine
reflected in our window,
where it sought safety.

Sonnet

I scan your features, your paused eyes,
calm below the rafters of night,
as a strenuous car scolds a far rise,
edges through dark, a wistful kite.
It may confound the dizzy night to think –
since thoughts can make things true –
the moon will land, stir a landscape's ink,
tell old tales, talk them through.

Thousands of such nights have we lain
side by side, though our looks have flown,
and now so close, I hear his name
from the dark of years, a boy once known.
Who guards the secrets of your old life
you gave up for me, sweet wife?

Ma 間

*Thirty spokes meet in the hub, though the space
between is the essence of the wheel* – Lao Tzu

She talks less now – where to start? –
voicing the worst discomforts,
may bait a hook with an old husk

of anecdote, that most swim past.
As if to improvise bridges
over the flow of predictable days,

young nurses in twos or threes
talk through their foreign trips, and
when they're off again. Outside,

a visitor locks his sequential life
in the car park. On the back seat, files,
in the boot, samples. Now,

he leans in with a small gift,
adjusting his words
to the guessing game with her,

since she found a forest in her head,
and her thoughts spread
in the shifting light of a mist.

Some days still,
she's a Japanese garden:
her arms outstretched like branches,

conspicuously held from earth
by her cane's wooden stay,
paths shrunk to stepping stones.

He talks, knows nothing of Japan,
yet is gently possessed by gaps,
by intervals, by stillnesses –

Ma 間, the *space between*,
differently conscious of its place,
filling in days, making up the whole.

Mind the gap

At the market,   a sudden opportunity
    beside the dart-like silvery fish;
    you feel you want to shake his hand
ask him how he's doing   look him straight in the eyes.
Say welcome to the club
        of *former* something or others,
now he's up the proverbial creek of the final lost election.

And you want   to see what was forbidden before,
ask him if he'll take a sabbatical
        or a break from it all,
to go where lights pearl along   a once-in-a-lifetime seafront
        like a charm bracelet.

You sense a seller's market,   one you have longed to corner:
    the market of being human ...
so, you move closer to unfold an idea,   touch his sleeve,
    reach an exposed part   to tell him
        through one single look
how you understand the politicians
                and their spin doctors,
with their climbed viewpoints, assured sightings,
who put on faces   for every ambition,
        but are sentenced to believe.

And how   no creed ever allows for remorse.
        But
        failing more is existing more...
The unhappy ones alone
think they can go back.

All clear

No-one talks except the staff,
    trained to overcompensate.
A nurse fills out my details.
    I give her papers, raw data,
minus all the blazing dawns and dusks
    of every moment counts,
then sit among zipped faces
    in the small, resonant silence
they've wrapped in coats. Where are we
    when we are not yet called?

I think of the traffic on the way in,
    the proliferation of speed bumps
we learn to see coming,
    then centre on the narrative text:
the MRI scan will be me again
    with different words. I'll take
the poor pastiche anyhow if it flatters,
    with no blobs or splotches, or
at worst, a smear with a known name,
    a telltale with a stutter.

A man is leaning, elbows on knees,
    searching, abdicating his thoughts.
A thread of an infant unravels hopefully,
    her mother pulls her back
onto a single purpose seat. So,
    living is long, bland, staggered,
stretching like an unworldly peace
    where everyone has their turn.

Finally, mine is up,
    the doctor's back and I can go.
There's the one intact moment
    when he forces a smile,
hands me my X-ray – that thin acetate
    which thieves open doors with.

Brain surgery on prime time

It came knocking on her door...

In for a rough ride, she sits in a carwash,
water coming down like a stage curtain,
hugging the shore of her handbag.

He drives now. From her passenger seat,
she waves, blows kisses to her kids
at the school gate before they vanish.

It's time: she clasps a bed's side-rail
and evening sky flushes a warning red.
The surgeon hovers over a chart

as if readying a ping-pong serve.
Body-talking, she holds his look
and her husband's packed hand.

The last scant meal delivered –
in the saving business too. Come dawn,
she hears voices in the unloading bay.

Whichever way the skull is sliced
she must talk through it all:
humanity's ten-thousand-year-old gift,

even counting gently up to ten.
Words must hold like stars
in the infinity of a cerebrum,

the surgeon lost in his telescope.
She senses the edges of the cosmos
are long plastic wraps. Later,

a hint of ceiling racing past,
thin air snaking over her skin,
a door's atomic blast. Shapes

lean in like branches among
sprigs of tubes. A question
elbows through the foliage:

… who's there?

Shorthand Hotel

```
Brand new morning,         visitation of lit curtains,
    draw them,             inaugurate a back wall
like a right arrangement       of hindsight.
Then          a flood of silence,
a play of drops, a towel       eating into my senses.

Stepping down to breakfast     floorboards purr
    guests whisper like leaves,
choices break surface     from the land's knuckles.
         Absolute verge of things.
The table linen           deftly adorns
the strands of who we are.
      The day is toying with syntax.
Trees in the park nimbly        shred shafts
of sunlight             like purposeful shutters.

There's the owl in us      when owl there is:
the two-seventy-degree swivel.         Not
    the great-height verdict,          nor
the fierce bereaving           all night long,
hitched to an unerring oracle,         not
    a triggered shadow of wing
         obliterating the moon,
                   nor
the tiny lid squeak       of a rodent.
Not that.
```

The jar

i.m Irena Sendlerowa, Warsaw

She chose an apple tree with uncertain fruit
under which to bury the handwritten names.

Nights, the sky lit up unpredictably
over her street and garden, as if to say

no one day in history ever sobers up tolerably
to let us walk a thousand straight lines.

Saving children was not enough, not even
the 2500 she'd smuggled from the ghetto

who were taught to pray like good Catholics.
Just what is a life worth which leaves no trace

for a family waiting on a sign? Or with what
the Gestapo planned for her own:

crippled by torture in a dark cell, sentenced
to die, the file closed. Thus, she plotted out

her after-death: a digger years on,
clawing a car park's foundations perhaps,

hitting the jar of names, climbing down,
pulling out the damp, tacky pages

gleaned by ordinary miracle from
the softwood fibres of an age-old forest.

Simone Veil lays a foundation stone for a hospital, 1976

1/
as mother housewife Minister of Health before presiding
Europe / she soothes cement as if it's a baby's bawling / you
wonder who the baby is / faces shove and jostle to the bait of
a camera / the *Préfet* oozes a compliment / how well

she trowels / *I learnt that in the camps so I'm good at it / it was
my task* / said for the very first time / ah! nods the *Préfet* / a
ceremonial pin drops / such unknowing is bottomless / has
no echo / thus a foundation stone / to steady thoughts / to

answer how / the tender the contractor the local authority the future sick / that's where the fight is / inside heads
/ build as if the edifice will do its own shaping of us / and
don't think bricks are secondary / or walls protection enough

2/
the Gestapo at sixteen / her childhood games hijacked / the
painting by numbers / yellow stars as cat's cradles / optical
illusions with stripes / Chinese whispers in shivering queues
/ endless murmuring about jump rope / thirty entire years /

in that one day she trowelled the stone / that's what leading
a life means / now she enters the *Pantheon* / Paris is sweltering / layers of ceremony cushion of time / tell that to the
parents fanning their kid's faces / and cling to the inner voice
of how

/ how to be a witness / to a witness / how to pile up a single
life / after mounds of suitcases shoes glasses teeth / how
to cultivate rage / her coffin passes / we watch in lines /
stripped ourselves now / used to be cold and lice / call it this
time a cortege

Golem

It grunted only, one word – אמת, truth – pinned to its forehead, ineffable holy names on the parchment in its mouth. Moulded from the loam of the Vltava river to ward off the return of pogroms. But it shuffled around as if it had a will of its own, kept growing bigger, more cumbersome, failing to respect the Shabbat, elbowing scholars in their shuckling, frightening small children under their bed covers. Single-mindedness? A monster. One day, Rabbi Loew asked it to bend down to tie his laces. He knew the hidden in the language of the revealed, plucked one letter from the word: so, truth became מת, death. It returned to clay. I closed the book, shelved it.

Later, sleep's frontier. A nightmare frisking me. I recognise my friend waiting for me in a corner of a hall. He knows what I know, says nothing. Once I had not been there for him. He turns, lowers his eyes, and I am instantly a bending Golem. I wake with a start. Every night, the furious pyrotechnics of rewiring: displacing, projecting, compartmentalising. How true then can I be? Four o'clock, I grope through night's dark folds to the kitchen, switch on a light, eyes stinging. Should I get back in touch with him? After so long? I picture that single letter floating delicately down, like all the faded post-its on my fridge door I had stopped remembering.

Trojan horses

Convoluted,
that way to win back
a lady, born of a swan.
They readily opened the gate,
were taken in themselves.

Like all the Trojan horses
ever since, that we admitted:
in the tritium of piddle today
leaking from a power plant,
in particulates from exhausts,
thickening the cold air, in
neonicotinoids riding the pollen,
looping like a rodeo hat
in a loose hand.

Befuddled bees
tapping against our windows
over-punctuate our world.

And now,
to think backwards
out of the near-inextricable progress
we crouch inside.

Now,
to beat right time
for migrant birds taking wing
for hibernators in circadian tunnels
and for each rarer bee droning by,
which saves the empire too.
How?

By dancing.

True north

Evenings she's there, discreet,
a waif with a vacant look, drifting in
it seems from down the street.
A movement in air alerts my ear
when day has dropped its load
and closes in to overhear.

Mostly, she stands as if ready.
But for what? Her head lowered
who can guess what's never said?
My back turned, she fills the scene,
makes faces for a crowd of trees:
a pantomime soul, Columbine.

Her hair needs a comb and brush
and her frame, more flesh; how
I wish she would just grow up
and leave... not linger under the kite
of moon whose tugging smiles
she tries on, night after night.

Friends never see her frame
when they call in with bottles
that pop and hold such storms.
They think she's an uneasy idea,
hastily change the subject
for both of us no doubt to hear.

But they weren't there when your look
searched mine for true north.
Stillborn, in the doctor's book.
I held your hand to make us safe,
to find a key, that one door closed,
as the hoarded idea became waif.

Cardea

Roman goddess of hinges

What's worse, the storm or
the ominous lull beforehand?
Who cares where it springs from
when it's suddenly upon us?
I hurt you, turning away,
turning thunderously back,
not hearing you out, then
inveighing like the Almighty.

Swept by words into what
we are not – cliffs running
the edge of the rest of ourselves –
yet sheepish afterwards
among the clinking of spoons,
the echo of our teacups.

Ditch the master plan for loving,
take it faithfully apart. Instead,
we need the gods of all the tiny things,
for the million right moments
to close a door
to open a door.

The government of mud

The downpour ricochets off tarmac.
As we run, we're hunchbacked
afraid of taking off in puddles
or sliding on something beastly
like slugs with their joke name,

rising in viscous, raw, umber brown
as their mulch floods. They stretch
slowly, lower bodies honeycombed
like morel mushrooms, compelling
attention from thrushes.

Indoors we pant, towel-rub our hair,
beads running down our faces as years would,
yet are washed backwards into ourselves,
giggling at remembered scenes
before hot chocolate.

The world dries. Slugs, striped now
like the belly of blue whales,
survive by friction. Flat worms are
white lies, bits of old used string,
drowning in puddles for lack of grip.

Breakfast protocol

Once, the fine sand grains
cupped footprints,
shapes of courtship, play-castle moats,

contours hinting at a nucleus
of families.
They lay together ocean-bonded,

progeny from a long lineage,
raised as cliffs,
educated as shingle, grown up refined.

Now, in single file they fall,
fall apart –
that is not what I meant, at all –

their elocution laboured
in the divide and rule
their world has come to.

Turned upside down, the timer
does its neat
rounding off with double parentheses.

On its worthy own,
an egg
stresses to stranded hardness.

The pathetic fallacy

As if all one's life an anchor, pulling
in an offshore mooring, though
waves buffet the rock pools where
curious people take to drowning.

For a grieving infant all at sea,
a true prop is a lumpy hamster
in a cardboard shoe-box, a tribute
of dandelion, a lolly-stick cross.

Or your loved one's childhood doll
tearing you from her intimacy,
more versed in confidences and robes
than any striving priest.

The lamp I bought my dying mother,
the guitar of my confessions, the armchair
for life's blade: goodbye slouching friend,
soothe my body to the junkyard gate...

Bystanders which stop bystanding
as the world empties of people
as if trespassing on private land,
whispering to me *I am here* and

this is what you've become. So, I plead
the ontology of objects in an era
of packaging. No one can tell me that
an out-of-touch friend's sudden gift

is not alive with wonder. Or, when my
forefinger lightly pulls, the earnest photo
fallen from a never-finished book
is not half my wrestled life.

Crossed paths

Beara peninsula, Ireland

I follow the rudimentary track signs
leading towards the promontory head

where white ruffs choke the last rocks
and seals sign off with calligraphy.

Houses fall away, stone-walled fields
have set the land like place mats

for a forgotten meal, where rain
and squalls drub the earth to send folk

running for cover holding their hats,
or would do, had they come.

At a remote house with sunken thatch,
a last man nods to my curt wave.

He stands, watches my passing as if
losing another son who won't return.

I crease the map till the map runs out
then think of him and why I never asked

the way or stood before him simply,
seeking his help. First stars appear

their light comes askew too, tugged by
orbiting, the long way back to me.

Pantheon

A parked car, windows open,
the unbottled genie of mist... I followed
the manly voices, tightened by cold,

to a short pier on the still Lough Owel.
All four were treading water.
I asked the temperature. *Noine degrees!*

One with rubber gloves tossed a pebble
to his setter, springing above them
on the pier, in two minds, suspicious.

It's good for you, you should try it...
gifting the ninety-nine per cent of life left to try.
I pointed. What's on that island?

A church. Are there services? *Oh yeah,
you can swim there.* Swimming to church?
One shrugged, basking in the higher temple

of his own body. Can I take a picture?
Well quick, we cum out after fifteen minutes.
I see your legs are going white already.

You wanna see me ass! No, I don't...
So I left them, chased by their laughter,
as the genie fastened over the water,

the River Suck callows, the headstones,
all the way to Galway, where bars
tunnelled into night and fiddlers
reeled almighty to the last notes.

Would you recall?

We missed the boat to the Skellig Islands
rising from waves like clenched fists,
never climbed to the bee-hive huts,

the early monastery, its shattered walls
where men were torn from earth
through timeless prayer, lived beside

razorbill, the black-legged kittiwake,
unfathomable ocean. Our long walk,
the remote Dingle beach, our car

left by itself on an afterthought of tarmac
a flung wind lashing the marram grasses,
flapping our collars. A single gull

was knitting waves and they rolled in
in unyielding lines of white foam. And
like a dog impatient to slip its leash, our

laughter tore loose from the unruly trinity:
what's manifest, what's gone, what
vanishes then waits, for years.

Confirm Humanity

Before we subscribe you, we need to confirm
you are a human

Again!? For this online poetry site
I am asked to type in twig letters –
a crude barcode of my shelf life –
to display the gondola of my thoughts.

… Instantly it's as if I am back
in the blanket bogs
of the Maumturk Mountains
driving to a poetry reading.
Drizzle has drenched rushes
and moor grass into pastel,
mist has so clouded the land
sheep barely stain into it,
mountains are rubbed out, like
elementary school mistakes.

Laggard mist: a bully hovering
by the roadside silencing
the birds… just me now
feeling called to feed a cuckoo.
But there on a near bend,
hooked into space – like
torn fleece on a wire –
an unlikely idea passes, line
after emergent line, ruminant
yet to turn its head…

So, I'll click the self-fulfilling
prophecy. Human then
but with wadding. Contents
may have settled in transit.

Coda

Some people do that
when the time has come, tidying
what languished in cupboards,

sifting photos, papers, memorabilia,
traces of relationships, all that
the children should or needn't see.

Others who spoke too much, too little
when falling out, and still hoping
the better half makes a good whole,

trim their lines,
commit to a letter, balance
on a tongue what counts,

straight like a surgeon's words,
solitary like a drunkard's,
late decisions shelved for years.

Some things are swallowed
others put under a stone, but
most take to air like ring doves.

You may just remember
having seen them gaze into space
as if over a wide, open sea,

but no-one fathoms them really,
those deckhands looking on
as they scuttle their ships.

About the author

Christopher M James, a dual British/French citizen, was born and raised in West London. After university studies in English and Philosophy (and later Applied Linguistics) he embarked on a lifelong career abroad, first in teaching and then as a Human Resource professional in prominent international companies. He has lived and worked most notably in France, Italy and Thailand. Apart from his professional publications, his exclusive focus on poetry came with retirement. He is also a musician and some would say a failed journalist, and despite lifelong interests in current affairs, justice and human rights, he finds writing poetry the purest form of living in the present moment. Entwining strands of all these influences can be found throughout his writing. He founded and runs the French Online Poetry Stanza, and lives in the Perigord Noir, Dordogne.

He can be contacted at *ohmercy5@yahoo.fr*